Who Is Bob Dylan?

Who Is Bob Dylan?

by Jim O'Connor
illustrated by John O'Brien

Penguin Workshop

To Jane, who is everything to me—JOC

For my favorite niece, Hannah—JOB

PENGUIN WORKSHOP
An Imprint of Penguin Random House LLC, New York

Published by Penguin Workshop, an imprint of Penguin Random House LLC, New York.
PENGUIN and PENGUIN WORKSHOP are trademarks of Penguin Books Ltd.
WHO HQ & Design is a registered trademark of Penguin Random House LLC.
Printed in the USA.

Visit us online at www.penguinrandomhouse.com.

Library of Congress Control Number: 2013938960

ISBN 9780448464619 15 14 13 12

Contents

Who Is Bob Dylan?

On Mother's Day, 1946, a four-year-old boy wanted to sing a special song to his grandmother. He had practiced it and now he was ready. But all the grown-ups in the room were laughing and talking. No one was paying attention to him.

Finally Bobby Zimmerman had had enough. He stamped his foot on the floor until all the grown-ups stopped talking.

"If everybody in this room will keep quiet, I will sing for my grandmother. I'm going to sing 'Some Sunday Morning.'" When he finished, the grown-ups clapped and cheered for the little boy. So Bobby decided to sing the only other song he knew. There was more applause and cheering from all his relatives. Bobby liked it.

Sixty-six years later, in 2012, President Barack Obama presented the Medal of Freedom to Bobby Zimmerman. By then, he was known as Bob Dylan. The Medal of Freedom is the highest award given to people who are not soldiers. The little boy had become one of the most famous singers and songwriters in the world.

"There is not a bigger giant in the history of American music," the president said. "He is still chasing that sound, still searching for a little bit of truth. And I have to say that I am a really big fan."

How did Robert Allan Zimmerman become Bob Dylan? Who is the real Bob Dylan? He is many things. A singer, a songwriter, an actor, an author, a filmmaker.

Bob Dylan is also one of the most private people in the world. Unlike many famous people, he wants to keep who he is a secret.

Chapter 1
Hibbing

Robert Allan Zimmerman was born in Duluth, Minnesota, on May 24, 1941. His parents were Abe Zimmerman and Beatrice "Beatty"

Stone. In 1946 Bob's younger brother, David, was born. That same year Abe Zimmerman caught polio, a disease that left him with a limp.

Abe survived but was very sick for a long time. The Zimmermans decided to move to Hibbing, Minnesota. It was Beatty's hometown. Her family could help out while Abe slowly recovered.

Hibbing was a small town in a part of northern Minnesota called the "Iron Range." The mining of iron ore was the biggest industry. Abe ran a small furniture and appliance store there.

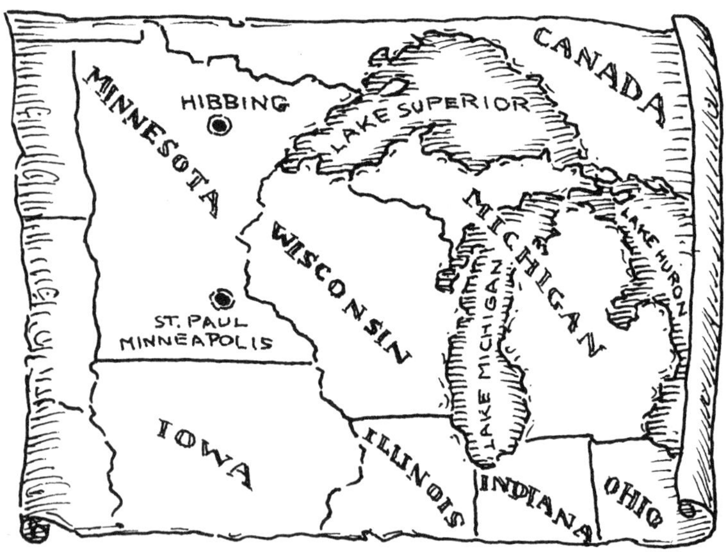

When Bob Zimmerman was growing up in Hibbing, there were only sixteen thousand people living there. Everyone knew everyone else. No one wanted to stand out or be different. On Sundays, most families went to church. The Zimmermans were among the few Jewish families. Bobby Zimmerman studied Hebrew and was bar mitzvahed when he was thirteen. That is a ceremony that celebrates a Jewish boy becoming a man.

But just three years later, Bob began to tell friends that he was not Jewish. He also began to make up stories about himself. He said he had run away from home many times. Not true. He said he had worked in a circus. Not true. Later he began to tell people that he was an orphan. Absolutely not true. Why did he make up these stories? Maybe he thought they made him seem more interesting. Maybe he had reasons for hiding his true identity.

At ten Bob decided to learn to play a musical instrument. His cousin gave him one piano lesson before Bob announced that he would teach himself. And he did!

But what kind of music would he play? In the early 1950s, few teenagers in Hibbing listened to a new kind of music called rock and roll. The local radio station in Hibbing was, like the town itself, conservative and dull. None of the music it played

appealed to Bob. At night he could listen to radio stations from as far away as Louisiana. He loved the mix of gospel music, blues, and black rhythm and blues.

He heard music that he liked on TV, too. In 1952 Abe Zimmerman brought home one of Hibbing's first TV sets. Bob and his friends couldn't get enough of it. Soon they would be able to watch Westerns like *Gunsmoke* and comedies like *I Love Lucy* and *The Honeymooners*.

On Sunday nights everyone watched *The Ed Sullivan Show*, a tremendously popular variety show. Bob saw early rock groups like Bill Haley and the Comets, and Elvis Presley. On September 9, 1956, one of Presley's first songs on *The Ed Sullivan Show* was "Ready Teddy" by Little Richard.

Little Richard was a black singer. Bob had heard his hit song "Tutti Frutti." Little Richard's pounding piano and wild screaming bowled Bob over. When he started playing piano, Bob copied Little Richard's stand-up style of playing.

EARLY ROCK LEGENDS

THE THREE MOST INFLUENTIAL ROCK MUSICIANS OF THE 1950S AND EARLY '60S WERE LITTLE RICHARD, CHUCK BERRY, AND ELVIS PRESLEY.

RICHARD WAYNE "LITTLE RICHARD" PENNIMAN WAS BORN ON DECEMBER 5, 1932, IN MACON, GEORGIA. A GREAT SHOWMAN, HE OFTEN PLAYED PIANO STANDING UP, POUNDING ON THE KEYS. HIS HIT SONGS INCLUDE "TUTTI FRUTTI," "LONG TALL SALLY," AND "GOOD GOLLY, MISS MOLLY."

HE WAS HEAVILY INFLUENCED BY GOSPEL MUSIC. THIS IS THE KIND OF MUSIC SUNG IN AFRICAN AMERICAN CHURCHES. AT ONE POINT HE QUIT ROCK AND ROLL AND BECAME A MINISTER.

LITTLE RICHARD WAS INDUCTED INTO THE ROCK AND ROLL HALL OF FAME IN 1986 AND THE SONGWRITERS HALL OF FAME IN 2003.

LITTLE RICHARD

CHUCK BERRY

CHARLES EDWARD ANDERSON "CHUCK" BERRY WAS BORN ON OCTOBER 18, 1926, IN ST. LOUIS, MISSOURI. SOME OF HIS MOST FAMOUS SONGS ARE "MAYBELLENE," "ROLL OVER, BEETHOVEN," "ROCK AND ROLL MUSIC," AND "JOHNNY B. GOODE."

HIS DISTINCTIVE GUITAR PLAYING HAS BEEN IMITATED BY ALMOST EVERY ROCK GUITAR PLAYER IN HISTORY. HIS SONGS WERE SO POPULAR AND SO WELL KNOWN THAT HE COULD PLAY WITH A LOCAL BAND ANYWHERE AND BE SURE THEY WOULD KNOW HIS MUSIC.

THE BEATLES PLAYED MANY OF HIS SONGS IN THEIR EARLY DAYS. THEY PUT "ROCK AND ROLL MUSIC" AND "ROLL OVER, BEETHOVEN" ON THEIR EARLY ALBUMS. HE WAS VOTED INTO BOTH THE ROCK AND ROLL HALL OF FAME AND THE SONGWRITERS HALL OF FAME IN 1986.

EARLY ROCK LEGENDS

ELVIS AARON PRESLEY WAS BORN IN TUPELO, MISSISSIPPI, ON JANUARY 8, 1935. HIS FAMILY SOON MOVED TO MEMPHIS, TENNESSEE, WHICH WAS HIS HOME FOR THE REST OF HIS LIFE. EVERY YEAR HUNDREDS OF THOUSANDS OF FANS STILL VISIT HIS MANSION, GRACELAND.

ELVIS FIRST RECORDED FOR SUN RECORDS IN MEMPHIS. SAM PHILLIPS, SUN'S OWNER, WANTED ELVIS TO BRING BLACK RHYTHM AND BLUES TO WHITE AUDIENCES. UNLIKE LITTLE RICHARD AND CHUCK BERRY, ELVIS DID NOT WRITE HIS OWN SONGS. HE PLAYED GUITAR ONSTAGE AND IS CREDITED WITH MAKING THE GUITAR, AND NOT THE PIANO, THE LEAD INSTRUMENT IN ROCK AND ROLL.

UNTIL THE ARRIVAL OF THE BEATLES, ELVIS WAS THE MOST FAMOUS SINGER IN THE WORLD. HE DIED ON AUGUST 16, 1977, AT AGE FORTY-TWO. HE, TOO, WAS INDUCTED INTO THE ROCK AND ROLL HALL OF FAME IN 1986. OVER 2.5 BILLION OF ELVIS'S RECORDS HAVE BEEN SOLD WORLDWIDE.

ELVIS PRESLEY

Chapter 2
A Cool Guitar

At about the same time he started listening to rock, Bob decided to learn guitar. His parents rented one for him. Bob taught himself to play with a book that showed the basic chords. He spent hours practicing and trying out different kinds of sounds.

Soon Bob wanted a cooler and better guitar. He had his eye on a flashy guitar from a catalog. It was turquoise with a white wing painted near the strings and cost thirty-nine dollars. (That was a lot of money in the 1950s.)

He knew his parents would not understand why he wanted to spend so much money on a guitar. So Bob saved up twenty dollars for the down payment. By doing this, he could take the guitar home. However, until he had completely paid for it, he kept the guitar hidden. Then he started playing it around the house. Bob's parents were impressed with how hard he'd worked to buy that guitar.

In high school, Bob and two friends formed a band called the Golden Chords. There was a drummer and a guitar player, and Bob played piano. The Golden Chords soon split up, and Bob formed another band with three other boys. This new, nameless band had electric guitars and very loud amplifiers. When Hibbing High sponsored a talent show, Bob and his friends signed up.

As soon as it was their turn, they turned the amplifiers as high as they would go. The music was so loud that no one could hear Bob singing.

After just a few minutes the principal cut the power. The nameless band left the stage.

In high school Bob was something of a loner. He kept to himself and seldom spoke up in class. Nor did he play any sports or join clubs, not even the school band. He preferred practicing his guitar on his own, or drawing and writing poems.

Still, Bob found ways to be noticed. He talked his father into buying him a Harley-Davidson motorcycle. Bob wore a black leather jacket and had a cute girlfriend who rode on the back of the bike while he roared around Hibbing.

The girl's name was Echo Star Helstrom. She was Bob's first real girlfriend. Echo's family was less well off than the Zimmermans. Her family lived in a tiny house outside of town. Bob's family was middle class and had a nice house in a nice neighborhood.

But Echo and Bob shared much in common. They both loved listening to the Louisiana radio stations late at night. Echo was as crazy about rock and roll and rhythm and blues as he was. Like Bob, she didn't fit in at high school. They both wanted to get out of Hibbing as soon as they graduated.

Bob was already planning a new identity for himself. Changing his last name was part of the plan. Echo was the first person to hear his new name: Bob Dillon. There was a popular TV character called Matt Dillon on *Gunsmoke*. But Bob told people that he chose the name because he had an uncle named Dillon who was a gambler in Las Vegas. That wasn't true. There was no uncle named Dillon anywhere. A couple of years later Bob changed the spelling of his new last name to D-y-l-a-n.

Some people thought that Bob had picked the name Dylan because of the famous Welsh poet Dylan Thomas. But Bob denied that, too. Like with so many other parts of the Bob Dylan story, he offered no explanation at all.

In June 1959, Bob graduated from high school. Under his yearbook picture it said that his ambition was "to join Little Richard."

Robert Zimmerman: to join "Little Richard"—
Latin Club 2; Social Studies Club 4.

BOB DYLAN'S ALIASES

BOB DYLAN HAS WORKED UNDER MANY DIFFERENT NAMES. AMONG THEM ARE:

- ***BLIND BOY GRUNT***—PERFORMER ON THE *BROADSIDE BALLADS, VOL. 1* COMPILATION ALBUM (1963)
- ***BOB LANDY***—PLAYED PIANO ON *THE BLUES PROJECT* COMPILATION ALBUM (1964)
- ***BOO WILBURY***—PERFORMER ON THE SECOND TRAVELING WILBURYS ALBUM (1990)
- ***ELMER JOHNSON***—APPEARED IN CONCERT WITH THE BAND (1969)

- ***ELSTON GUNN***—PIANO PLAYER BRIEFLY ON TOUR WITH BOBBY VEE (LATE 1950S)
- ***JACK FROST***—PRODUCER OF SEVERAL STUDIO ALBUMS (2001–2012)
- ***LUCKY WILBURY***—PERFORMER ON THE FIRST TRAVELING WILBURYS ALBUM (1988)

- ***ROBERT MILKWOOD THOMAS***—CONTRIBUTED PIANO AND VOCALS TO STEVE GOODMAN'S ALBUM *SOMEBODY ELSE'S TROUBLES* (1973)
- ***SERGEI PETROV***—COWRITER OF THE FILM *MASKED AND ANONYMOUS* (2003)
- ***TEDHAM PORTERHOUSE***—HARMONICA PLAYER ON RAMBLIN' JACK ELLIOTT'S ALBUM *JACK ELLIOTT* (1964)

As a graduation gift, Bob got a collection of folk records. When he started listening to them, Bob came across a black folksinger named Huddie "Lead Belly" Ledbetter.

Lead Belly's music amazed and excited Bob. He had never heard anything like it.

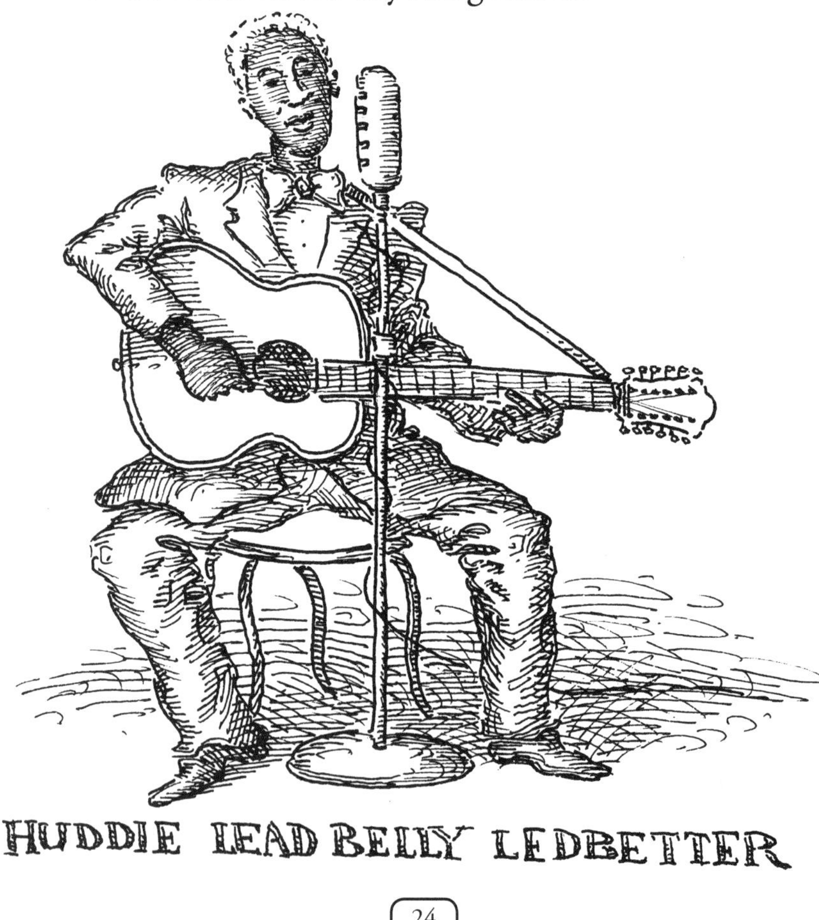

HUDDIE LEAD BELLY LEDBETTER

Lead Belly had written hundreds of songs. "Good Night, Irene" became a number one hit on the radio in 1950 when it was recorded by a group of folksingers called the Weavers. The Weavers were a white group. Black musicians were not played on most radio stations.

Lead Belly's main instrument was the twelve-string guitar. Bob called a high school friend and said, "I've discovered something great!"

By this time Bob and Echo were no longer a couple. Bob had been seeing other girls. Echo was furious and told Bob they were through.

Echo would always be special to Bob. A few years later he wrote a song called "Girl from the North Country." Many people believe that it is about Echo.

Chapter 3
Dinkytown

The University of Minnesota in Minneapolis was Bob's ticket out of Hibbing. He was not much interested in college. But Abe and Beatty expected him to earn a degree and then return home. Perhaps he'd go into business with his father. That's what they hoped, at least.

Bob had scouted out the university long before he enrolled. During his senior year in high school, he had talked his dad into buying him a used Ford. He would make the three-hour drive to Minneapolis and spend long weekends hanging out in a neighborhood near the university called Dinkytown.

During his first year of college, he spent more time at a coffeehouse called The 10 O'Clock Scholar than in classrooms. Playing and singing folk songs was not a popular pastime in 1959.

Most college kids liked smooth, bland singers like Pat Boone or groups like the Lettermen. The cooler students liked jazz. But there were only a few people in Dinkytown who were interested in folk music. One was "Spider" John Koerner.

He and Bob became friends. They both played guitar and were trying to write songs. Koerner thought that Bob had "a pretty voice," much different from the way he sounded later on.

FOLK SONGS

FOLK SONGS ARE THE AGE-OLD SONGS THAT PEOPLE FROM A CERTAIN AREA LEARN AS CHILDREN. THE SONGS ARE PASSED DOWN IN FAMILIES. THE LYRICS MAY CHANGE OVER TIME. EVERY COUNTRY HAS ITS OWN FOLK MUSIC. MEXICAN FOLK SONGS ARE VERY DIFFERENT FROM RUSSIAN FOLK SONGS.

A LOT OF AMERICAN FOLK SONGS COME FROM WEST VIRGINIA AND THE APPALACHIAN MOUNTAINS. PEOPLE FROM IRELAND AND ENGLAND SETTLED THIS PART OF AMERICA IN THE EIGHTEENTH AND NINETEENTH CENTURIES. THAT'S WHY MANY FOLK SONGS WERE ORIGINALLY ENGLISH OR IRISH SONGS. THEY OFTEN TELL A SAD STORY, MAYBE ABOUT HAVING YOUR HEART BROKEN OR BEING WRONGLY ACCUSED OF A CRIME.

DURING THE LATE 1950S AND EARLY 1960S, FOLK MUSIC BECAME VERY POPULAR IN THE UNITED STATES. YOUNG MUSICIANS LIKE BOB DYLAN STARTED WRITING NEW FOLK SONGS. THEY OFTEN HAD STRONG MESSAGES ABOUT CIVIL RIGHTS AND JUSTICE.

Bob was always reinventing his life story, telling his new friends wild tales. Often, one story contradicted another. After a while, folks in Dinkytown didn't take any of them seriously.

Soon Bob completely stopped going to class. He spent all of his time on his music. Bob was not a great guitar player yet. "Plenty of other kids were as good," a friend recalled. But "if you didn't see him for two weeks it would seem as if he'd made three years progress."

Bob performed at The 10 O'Clock Scholar, along with another local coffeehouse. Sometimes he might get paid ten dollars for playing all night. Other times he played for free. As long as there was an audience, he was happy.

All of Bob's Dinkytown friends loved folk music. Bob would listen to their records. When he heard someone he really liked, he would try to play and even sing like the performer.

For instance, Slim Harpo was a black blues singer. He played guitar and harmonica. Bob had been a very good harmonica player but had stopped to work on his guitar. A picture of Slim Harpo showed him with a wire holder around his neck to hold his harmonica. Bob made his own holder and began playing guitar and harmonica like Slim Harpo.

SLIM HARPO

At about the same time, Bob discovered Woody Guthrie. A friend loaned him a book that Guthrie had written about his life. It was called *Bound for Glory.* Guthrie had spent years crisscrossing the United States singing and writing folk songs. Many of his songs had a strong message. For instance, he thought a lot of poor people didn't have a chance for a decent life.

WOODY GUTHRIE

His most famous song is "This Land Is Your Land." The song describes a beautiful and bountiful United States. The message is that our country should provide for all Americans. Each chorus ends with the words

"This land was made for you and me." The song was written in 1940, when many people in the United States had no jobs or homes and were going hungry.

Guthrie sang with a strong Oklahoma accent. Within a few weeks, Bob was singing just like Woody.

Bob learned new songs by listening to records. At least once he stole records from a friend's apartment. Some were Woody Guthrie albums. It wasn't right, but that didn't stop him. When Bob's friend confronted him, he gave the records back and apologized. Their friendship ended that day.

"I think he believed that he needed [the records] more than I did," the man later said. "He had taken the very best of the lot."

As Bob's playing and songwriting grew stronger, he became more competitive with his friend Spider John. He wanted to be the best folkie in Dinkytown. Most people thought Spider

John would be famous long before Dylan. They were wrong.

By this time, Bob had decided that Dinkytown was not a big enough stage for him. He wanted to head east and find his hero, Woody Guthrie.

Chapter 4
Greenwich Village

Bob Dylan arrived in Greenwich Village in February 1961. Greenwich Village is a neighborhood in downtown Manhattan. It was the center of the folk music scene in the early 1960s.

Bob was nearly broke and had no place to stay. Sometime between leaving Minnesota and arriving in "the Village," Bob had taken on a new way of dressing. He wore dark blue jeans, denim or plaid wool shirts, a sheepskin coat, and a black corduroy hat with a little brim.

Bob Dillon from Dinkytown was gone.

MacDougal Street was the Main Street of Greenwich Village. The most popular folksingers played in clubs on MacDougal, such as The

MACDOUG

Commons, Cafe Wha?, and Gerde's Folk City. The most famous folksingers were Dave Van Ronk, Ramblin' Jack Elliot, Pete Seeger, Danny Kalb, and the Weavers. They all played at these clubs.

The community of singers was small and welcomed newcomers. Everyone liked Bob, and people went out of their way to help him. He had a place to stay and free meals right from the start.

Washington Square Park was like the town square of Greenwich Village. Folksingers met by

WASHINGTON SQUARE PARK IN GREENWICH VILLAGE

the big fountain in the middle of the park to play together.

Dave Van Ronk was like the mayor of MacDougal Street. He was a gifted guitar player with a deep, rough voice that made songs come alive. He recognized Dylan's talent immediately.

Bob spent a few weeks sleeping on Van Ronk's couch. The two became very close. Dave listened to all of Dylan's "life stories" and didn't believe most of them. Dave later told a writer, "We accepted him not because of the things he said he'd done but because we respected him as a performer. His pose didn't bother us. Whatever he said offstage, onstage he told the truth as he knew it."

DAVE VAN RONK

One of Van Ronk's signature songs was his arrangement of a folk song called "The House of the Rising Sun." Dylan copied Van Ronk's version of the song word for word and note for note. Later he put it on his first album, even though he knew Van Ronk was planning to record this song himself. Van Ronk felt betrayed and stopped talking to Bob for two months. Bob never said he was sorry.

Chapter 5
Suze

Soon Bob was playing in all the clubs. In July he was invited to play in a concert for WRVR-FM. The concert raised money for the radio station, which played a lot of folk music. The concert lasted twelve hours. Dylan got to do one set of five songs. He was in his Woody Guthrie phase and sang with Woody's Oklahoma twang.

Afterward Bob was introduced to Suze (pronounced Suzy) Rotolo. She was seventeen. He was twenty. Bob thought

that Suze was cool. She'd grown up in New York City, and her parents were civil rights activists.

Bob and Suze fell hard for each other. For the next two years, Suze would be the most important person in Bob's life. "Outside of my music," he wrote in his autobiography, *Chronicles: Volume One,* "being with her seemed to be the main point of my life. She was involved in the New York art scene, painted and made drawings for various publications, worked in graphic design and Off-Broadway theatrical productions, also worked on civil rights committees—she could do a lot of things."

Suze recognized Bob's talent and worked hard to help him get better known. She and her older sister, Carla, persuaded the owner of Gerde's Folk City to book Bob Dylan for two weeks. A good review of the first show appeared in the *New York Times*. There was even a photo of Dylan playing his guitar. A young singer couldn't ask for better publicity.

Curious folk fans packed Folk City to hear Bob. Just by chance, Bob got to meet a famous music producer. His name was John Hammond. Bob asked for a chance to play for him.

Hammond had a keen ear for talent. He had discovered musicians like Count Basie, Billie Holiday, Sonny Terry, Pete Seeger, and the folksinger Carolyn Hester. He decided to take a chance on Bob Dylan. Within the week, Bob signed a five-year contract with Columbia Records.

Some Village musicians were jealous of Dylan. How did this new kid merit a review in the *New York Times*? They also called him a "sellout" for signing a contract with a big company like Columbia. (A sellout is someone who will give up things he believes in just to make money.) Back in Dinkytown, his old friends couldn't believe what they read. How could Dylan have a record contract? He wasn't nearly as good as Spider John Koerner.

The first album was simply called *Bob Dylan*. The cover photo shows a very young but

confident Dylan staring into the camera. He is much skinnier than he was only a year earlier. His face is no longer round and chubby. He's wearing the black corduroy hat and holding his guitar. "Here I am," he seems to be saying. The only musician on it was Bob playing his guitar and harmonica. One song is written to Woody Guthrie.

Bob had met Woody Guthrie in February 1961. By that time, Woody was so sick that the great American singer and storyteller could not walk. His hands and shoulders shook, and he could barely talk.

Dylan played some of his songs for Woody. A few days later, Bob wrote "Song to Woody," which appears on the first album. So does "Highway 51." It is a long blues song that is more "talked" than "sung," just like some of Woody's best-known songs.

Bob Dylan was good for a first album. But he was young and unknown. The album was not a big hit. Even so, Bob was already working on his next album. The one that would make everyone sit up and notice him.

Chapter 6
Blowin' in the Wind

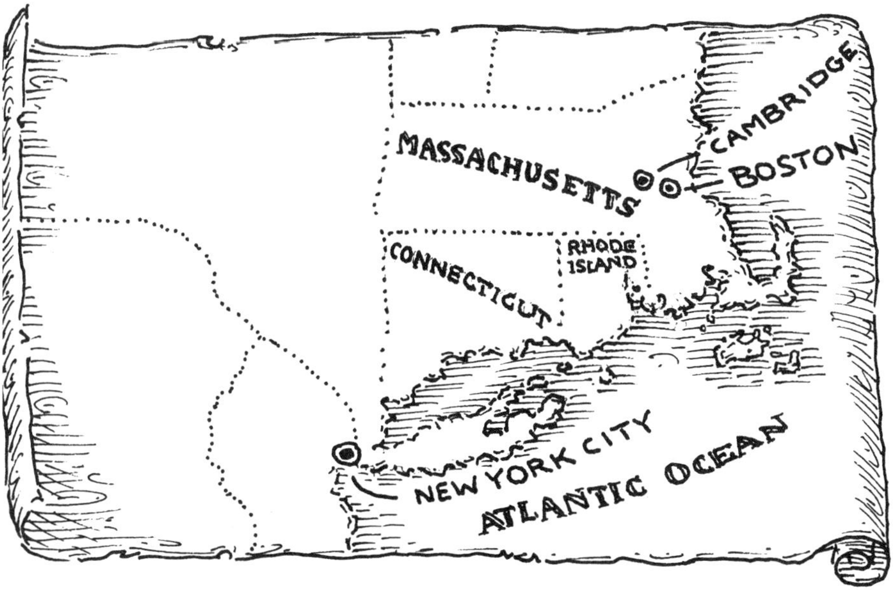

In 1961 Bob visited Cambridge, Massachusetts. It is a town right next to Boston, and the home of Harvard University. Cambridge's folk music community rivaled New York's. Joan Baez was the queen of the Cambridge folk scene. She had a perfect, pure soprano and sang traditional English and American songs. Her first three albums all went gold, selling more than five hundred thousand copies each.

Bob had first seen Joan on TV back in Minnesota. She had shiny black hair down to her waist. He wrote about his first impression of her in *Chronicles: Volume One:* "I couldn't stop looking at her, didn't want to blink. The sight of her made me sigh. All that and then there was the voice. She sang in a voice straight to God. Nothing she did didn't work."

Joan Baez was not impressed when she heard Dylan's first album. But her opinion changed two years later when she heard the song "Blowin' in the Wind." It is the first cut on Bob's second album, *The Freewheelin' Bob Dylan*. The song asks a series of questions that touch on war, civil rights, and injustice.

Each chorus ends "The answer my friend, is blowin' in the wind / The answer is blowin' in the wind." By that he meant that the answers to our problems were right in front of us, although we often could not see that.

Since it first came out, "Blowin' in the Wind" has been recorded by many musicians. Probably the most famous version is by the folksinging trio

Peter, Paul and Mary. Their recording shot to number two on the *Billboard* chart in 1963.

The cover of *The Freewheelin' Bob Dylan* featured a memorable photograph. Suze and Bob are walking down a wintery Greenwich Village street. They are huddled against the wind and look very young and in love.

Freewheelin' was an immediate success and brought Bob to the attention of folkies all across the United States. The release of the album in late May was part of a string of events that made Bob famous.

In 1962 he hired a new manager who got Bob a spot on *The Ed Sullivan Show* in May 1963. This was the big time! Bob was planning to perform "Talkin' John Birch

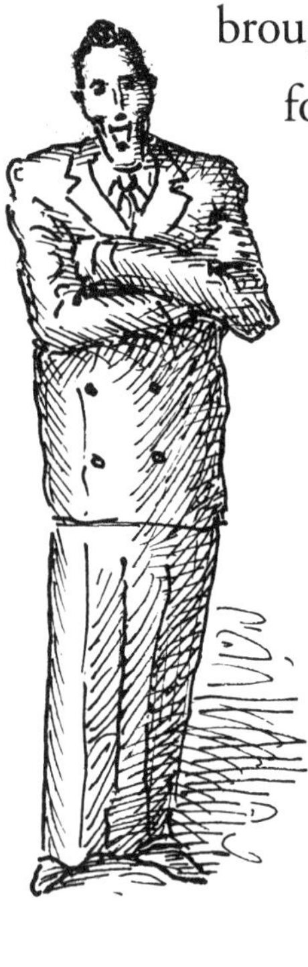

ED SULLIVAN

Society Blues." The song made fun of a small, very conservative group called the John Birch Society. He later changed the name of the song to "Talkin' John Birch Paranoid Blues." During rehearsals a CBS lawyer told Ed Sullivan that Bob couldn't sing the song. CBS was nervous that the John Birch Society might sue the network. When Ed Sullivan gave Bob the news, he blew up. He was being censored! Bob walked out of the television studio and went home.

This was great publicity for Bob. Musicians supported his walkout. Young people everywhere were impressed with Dylan for standing up for his beliefs.

The Ed Sullivan controversy won Bob some more fans, but the Newport Folk Festival in Rhode Island made him a star.

The Newport Festival was the place to hear the best folk music in the United States. By the time the 1963 festival began, Joan Baez had learned many of Dylan's songs and was a big fan. She invited Bob onstage and they sang two songs together. She was a superstar, and it was a very generous thing to do.

Bob also got to perform by himself at Newport. He was the very last act. Then all the famous singers came back onstage, joined hands, and sang the civil rights anthem "We Shall

Overcome." Bob was center stage with Joan Baez.

During that summer Suze and Bob split up. Bob was spending a lot of time with Joan, and Suze had had enough.

Later that summer, on August 28, 1963, almost three hundred thousand people gathered in Washington, DC, to take part in the March on Washington for Jobs and Freedom. Three quarters of the crowd were African Americans. Everyone was taking part in a rally for civil rights and equality for African Americans. In southern states in the early 1960s, most black people could not vote. They could not eat in the same restaurants as white people, or stay in the same hotels, or even use the same water fountains.

The marchers were voicing support for an important civil rights bill that they hoped Congress would pass. The bill would help to end unfair treatment of minorities.

Standing in front of the Lincoln Memorial, the Reverend Martin Luther King Jr. electrified the audience with his "I Have a Dream" speech.

Bob Dylan was one the many musicians who entertained the crowd that day. He sang several

songs, including "Only a Pawn in Their Game," which is about the murder of a civil rights leader named Medgar Evers.

A year later President Lyndon Johnson signed the Civil Rights Act of 1964, and in 1965 he signed the Voting Rights Act. These were major victories for the civil rights movement.

CIVIL RIGHTS MOVEMENT

THE CIVIL RIGHTS MOVEMENT HAD MANY GOALS. IT WANTED TO MAKE SURE AFRICAN AMERICANS HAD THE RIGHT TO VOTE, EAT IN ANY RESTAURANT, STAY IN ANY HOTEL, BUY A HOUSE IN ANY NEIGHBORHOOD, AND HAVE A FAIR CHANCE AT ANY JOB.

THE MOVEMENT BELIEVED IN PEACEFUL PROTESTS AND "CIVIL DISOBEDIENCE." FOR INSTANCE, BLACK TEENAGERS WOULD SIT IN WHITES-ONLY RESTAURANTS AND NOT BUDGE UNTIL THEY WERE SERVED OR TAKEN AWAY BY THE POLICE.

Bob Dylan first became famous for his protest songs. For a time, Bob Dylan took part in voter-registration drives and sit-ins. Yet, very soon after the March on Washington, he decided to stop writing protest songs. He was more interested in rock and roll. That's where he was headed.

Chapter 7
Changes

In February 1964, Bob and three friends set out in a Ford station wagon to see America. They planned to follow the same route as the writer Jack Kerouac did when he drove across country in 1948. Kerouac wrote about that trip in a popular novel, *On the Road*.

Bob wrote "Mr. Tambourine Man" and "Chimes of Freedom" while they drove to New Orleans and then on to San Francisco. Both songs were very different from his protest songs. Dylan was writing lyrics that read like poetry:

> Take me on a trip
> upon your magic swirlin' ship

My senses have been stripped,
my hands can't feel to grip.

Bob also started writing a novel called *Tarantula*. It wasn't like most novels. There was no plot. *Tarantula* was Dylan's dreamlike diary of his American journey. It was not published until 1971.

After he finished *Tarantula*, Bob wrote one of his greatest songs, "Like a Rolling Stone." It's like a six-minute musical sum-up of his novel. Dylan recorded it as a rock song. Columbia did not know what to make of it.

While driving across America, Bob and his friends heard the Beatles for the first time. The song was "I Want to Hold Your Hand." Bob was floored. "I knew they were pointing the direction of where music had to go." It was not the same direction as Bob was heading. But he understood why the Beatles were going to become such superstars.

THE BEATLES

The 1964 Newport Folk Festival featured a very different Bob Dylan. After just one year of fame, Dylan was sick of being the "voice of his generation."

Bob wanted to move on with his songwriting. He was tired of being tied to protest songs. He was tired of the constant criticism from the press, and even his fans. Some of them didn't even like

"Blowin' in the Wind." Others, including Joan Baez, only wanted songs like "Wind." Bob felt that everyone should just be content to listen to his music.

Many people considered Dylan's solo concert at Newport in 1964 to be a disaster. He was

nervous before the show and worried about how his new songs would go over with the crowd. But onstage he didn't act nervous. He acted mad. He sang "Mr. Tambourine Man" angrily. The song's beautiful melody was choppy and abrupt. Later, while singing another song, he turned his back on the crowd. None of his fans booed him, but they were clearly puzzled.

John Hammond watched from backstage. He couldn't believe it! Dylan owed his fans respect, and he wasn't showing it to them.

But that night Bob Dylan simply didn't seem to care.

Chapter 8
Bob Goes Electric

Bob put away his acoustic guitar and switched to a Fender Stratocaster electric guitar. For his next album, his studio band was a rock-and-roll band with a full rock drum set.

At the Newport Folk Festival in July 1965, Bob Dylan heard something he never had before—loud booing from the audience. Later, the story went around that the Newport crowd booed him because they did not expect Bob to come out with a rock band. That isn't true. Most fans knew that they were going to hear an "electric" Dylan. The real reason for their anger was that Dylan played a very short set.

Al Kooper, who played organ for Bob that day, told writer David Dalton, "The reason they booed

is because he only played for fifteen minutes, when everybody else played for forty-five minutes to an hour. They were feeling ripped off. They wanted more."

Bob returned to the stage carrying an acoustic guitar. Maybe he was trying to make peace with

the crowd. He played “Mr. Tambourine Man” and “It’s All Over Now, Baby Blue.” But then he walked off again.

Dylan did not return to the Newport festival for thirty-seven years.

ACOUSTIC VERSUS ELECTRIC

AN ACOUSTIC GUITAR HAS A HOLLOW WOODEN BODY AND SIX STRINGS. IT IS PLAYED BY STRUMMING OR PLUCKING THE STRINGS. SOUND IS PRODUCED BY THE VIBRATION OF A SOUNDING BOARD INSIDE THE GUITAR. THERE IS A ROUND OR OVAL-SHAPED HOLE IN THE TOP OF THE GUITAR THAT LETS THE SOUND OUT. ACOUSTIC GUITARS ARE SOMETIMES CALLED FOLK GUITARS.

ELECTRIC GUITARS USUALLY HAVE SOLID BODIES. THEY HAVE SIX METAL STRINGS THAT VIBRATE OVER ELECTRONIC PICKUPS. THE SOUND TRAVELS THROUGH A CORD TO AN AMPLIFIER. BOTH THE GUITAR AND THE AMPLIFIER HAVE KNOBS FOR ADJUSTING VOLUME.

THERE ARE ALSO BOTH ACOUSTIC AND ELECTRIC TWELVE-STRING GUITARS. THEY ARE NOT POPULAR, BECAUSE THEY ARE HARD TO TUNE AND THEIR NECKS HAVE A TENDENCY TO WARP. TWELVE-STRING GUITARS ARE GENERALLY USED TO PLAY RHYTHM, NOT LEAD PARTS.

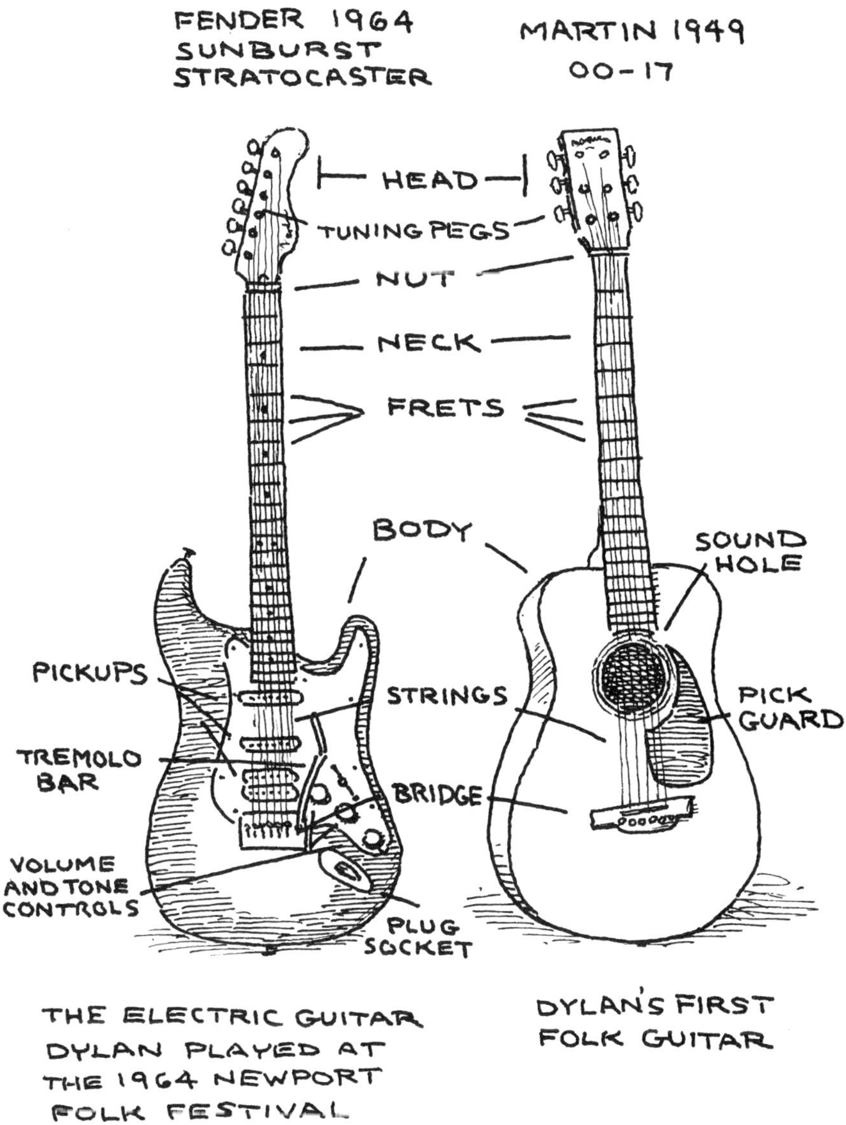
FENDER 1964
SUNBURST
STRATOCASTER
MARTIN 1949
00-17
HEAD
TUNING PEGS
NUT
NECK
FRETS
BODY
SOUND
HOLE
PICKUPS
STRINGS
PICK
GUARD
TREMOLO
BAR
BRIDGE
VOLUME
AND TONE
CONTROLS
PLUG
SOCKET
THE ELECTRIC GUITAR
DYLAN PLAYED AT
THE 1964 NEWPORT
FOLK FESTIVAL
DYLAN'S FIRST
FOLK GUITAR

That August, a new album called *Highway 61 Revisited* came out. The cover photo shows a different Dylan. He's wearing the kind of clothes rock singers wore in the sixties. He has on a wild purple and pink shirt over a Triumph Motorcycle T-shirt. He's holding sunglasses in one hand and looks ready to plug in and play rock music.

The album kicks off with "Like a Rolling Stone." The song's lyrics could be read as telling the folkie community that it wasn't very smart or cool. His music was changing.

In "Ballad of a Thin Man," Bob sings one of his most famous lines, "Because something is happening here / But you don't know what it is / Do you, Mr. Jones?" For years afterward, fans and interviewers would ask, "Who is Mr. Jones?" and "What does the line mean exactly?"

Bob Dylan has never said.

Chapter 9
Don't Look Back

Bob Dylan toured Great Britain in late 1965. Joan Baez was Bob's girlfriend and came on tour with him. It was his first time performing outside North America. He did eight shows. The documentary filmmaker D. A. Pennebaker

D.A.PENNEBAKER

followed Bob as he traveled around the country. He made a movie about Bob and the tour called *Don't Look Back*.

The film was released in 1967. It offered a candid look at a superstar. Bob Dylan comes across as cocky. He looks eager to poke fun at people who strike him as stupid, like a reporter from *Time* magazine.

During the tour, he also broke up with Joan Baez. Joan Baez was never as big a star in England as she was in America. She expected that Bob would bring her onstage during shows. After all, that's what she'd done when he was just starting out. But never once did he ask her to sing with him. In one of her last appearances in the film, she leaves Bob's hotel room while his friends snicker at her.

Don't Look Back was not a concert movie. Very little of the film showed Bob performing. Instead, it captured a very young man, not even

twenty-four years old, as he was becoming world famous.

Did being famous make Bob Dylan happy? It did not seem so. The album *Blonde on Blonde* came out right after the British tour. The cover photo showed Bob bundled up in a heavy coat with a checked scarf around his neck. Only three years had passed since Dylan was photographed with Suze on *The Freewheelin' Bob Dylan*. By now Bob looked a lot older and much less happy.

While some fans consider *Blonde on Blonde* Dylan's best album, one song on it came under attack. "Just Like a Woman" was criticized for making women look "greedy, whining and hysterical."

WOMEN'S LIB

THE WOMEN'S LIBERATION MOVEMENT—WOMEN'S LIB FOR SHORT—EMERGED IN THE EARLY 1960S. LIKE AFRICAN AMERICANS OF THE TIME, MANY WOMEN FELT THAT THEY WERE NOT TREATED FAIRLY. LEADERS OF THE MOVEMENT SUCH AS GLORIA STEINEM WANTED MORE WOMEN ADMITTED TO LAW SCHOOLS, BUSINESS SCHOOLS, AND MEDICAL SCHOOLS. THEY WANTED TO ELECT MORE WOMEN TO CONGRESS AND SEE MORE WOMEN APPOINTED JUDGES. WOMEN'S LIBBERS WANTED WOMEN TO GET PAID THE SAME AS MEN FOR DOING THE SAME JOB. AND THEY FELT HUSBANDS SHOULD SHARE IN HOUSEWORK AND HELP TO RAISE CHILDREN.

GLORIA STEINEM

VILLAGE GREEN, WOODSTOCK, NY

In the spring of 1966, Bob and another group, the Hawks (later renamed the Band), went on tour around the world together. It was exhausting. Afterward, Bob needed some time off. He went to the small village of Woodstock, New York. Bob had spent time in Woodstock in 1963 with Suze. It had been a happy time. She painted while he wrote songs. Woodstock held good memories for him.

The previous November, Bob had secretly married a woman named Sara Lownds. They had known each other for about a year. She was the same age as Bob and had grown up in Wilmington, Delaware. Her real name was Shirley. But her first husband convinced her to change it to Sara. Before meeting Bob, she had been a Playboy bunny and an actress. There are several stories of how they met—in high school (definitely not true), when she was a waitress (maybe), or when she was working for the filmmaker D. A. Pennebaker (most likely).

SARA LOWNDS

Bob enjoyed living in Woodstock. Almost no one knew that Bob was there. He could walk around town and not be bothered by anyone.

Then on July 29, 1966, something terrible happened. Bob was riding his motorcycle near his home. The back wheel of the bike suddenly stopped turning. Bob was thrown over the handlebars and seriously injured. Luckily Sara was driving right behind and took Bob to a nearby hospital.

WOODSTOCK

IN AUGUST 1969, A FARM IN UPSTATE NEW YORK BECAME THE SITE OF WHAT IS PROBABLY THE MOST FAMOUS ROCK-AND-ROLL FESTIVAL IN HISTORY. ALTHOUGH IT TOOK PLACE IN BETHEL, NEW YORK, IT ORIGINALLY WAS SUPPOSED TO BE HELD SIXTY MILES AWAY IN WOODSTOCK, NEW YORK. AND WOODSTOCK IS THE NAME THAT IT HAS ALWAYS BEEN KNOWN BY.

THE FESTIVAL LASTED FOR THREE DAYS. ABOUT FOUR HUNDRED THOUSAND YOUNG PEOPLE CAME, AND ALTHOUGH THERE WERE TERRIBLE STORMS, IT WAS A PEACEFUL, HAPPY TIME. THE WHO, JIMI HENDRIX, AND JANIS JOPLIN PLAYED THERE, AMONG OTHERS.

BOB DYLAN DID NOT PERFORM AT WOODSTOCK.

While Bob was recovering from the accident, he decided to stop performing. His manager had scheduled sixty concerts for him around the country. They were all canceled.

Bob wanted a change. He and Sara started a family, and it grew quickly. In addition to Sara's daughter from her earlier marriage, they had four children in five years: Jesse, Anna, Samuel, and Jakob. (Jakob is now the lead singer in the popular band the Wallflowers.)

"Having children changed my life and segregated me from just about everybody and everything that was going on," Bob wrote in *Chronicles: Volume One.* "Outside of my family, nothing held any real interest for me."

For the next few years Bob focused on his family. The Dylans moved from Woodstock to Greenwich Village, and eventually to Malibu, on the coast of southern California. Crazy fans and prying reporters, however, made it impossible for Bob and his family to have a "normal" life.

Chapter 10
Finding Faith

As Bob Dylan grew older and his family grew bigger, he began to look for more meaning in life. He became interested in his Jewish roots and what the religion meant.

Then Abe Zimmerman died of a heart attack in June 1968. In an interview in a Minnesota newspaper, Abe had talked about his famous son. His remarks were candid and sharp. "My son is a corporation and his public image is strictly an act . . . He wanted to be a folksinger, an entertainer. We couldn't see it, but we felt he was entitled to the chance. It's his life after all."

Bob was not happy with what his father said. Nevertheless, as soon as he heard the news of Abe's death, Bob went to Hibbing for the funeral.

He was deeply upset by his father's death. Bob was a parent now. So perhaps he understood how hard it was to be a father. He also made an effort to become closer to his mother and brother, David, again.

Bob and David spent time discussing the plans for their father's funeral. David was surprised that Bob still remembered the Hebrew prayer for the dead. The bar mitzvahed boy had not forgotten his religion.

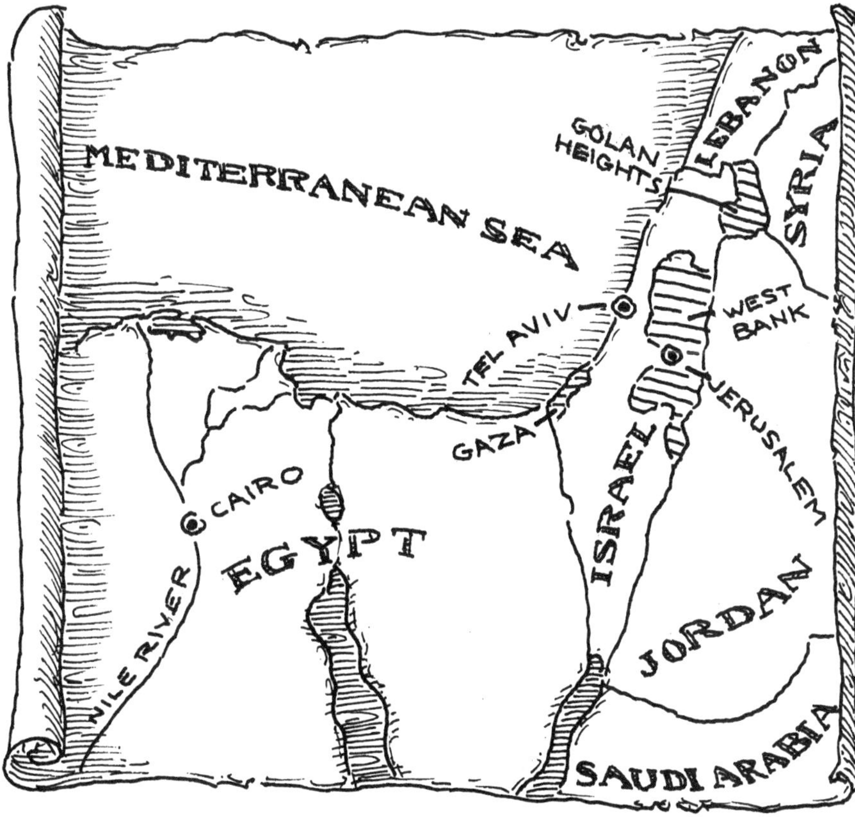

The following year Bob visited Israel. He went again in 1970 and in May 1971. During that visit, Bob and Sara visited the oldest parts of the city of Jerusalem. He told a rabbi there, "I'm a Jew. It touches my poetry, my life, in ways I can't describe."

A few days later Bob visited the Wailing Wall. For Jews, it is a very sacred place. People pray and leave written prayers stuck in the cracks of the wall. Someone snapped Bob's picture as he was praying at the Wall. It quickly appeared in newspapers around the world.

Rumors spread that Bob was thinking of moving his family to Israel. Other stories said they would live on a kibbutz or a farm. Or that they might buy an apartment in Jerusalem. In the end the stories turned out to be just stories.

Unfortunately, Bob's personal life unraveled over the next few years. His marriage fell apart. In 1977, Bob and Sara got divorced.

Once again Bob began touring the country. On November 18, 1978, he was onstage in Tempe, Arizona. Someone in the crowd could see that Bob was not feeling well and threw a silver cross to him. Bob picked it up and put it in his pocket.

The next night Bob was feeling even worse. In his pocket, he found the cross. That was what he needed, he believed, to feel better.

Right there in his hotel room, Bob had what he called a divine revelation. By that he meant that God was speaking to him. "The glory of the Lord knocked me down and picked me up," he said.

He became part of a Christian church in California. Several members of his band belonged to the same church.

His next three albums, *Slow Train Coming*, *Saved*, and *Shot of Love* had songs that explored Christian themes. Sometimes during concerts he would speak to the crowd about his new faith.

Many of his fans did not understand what was going on. Sometimes they would shout, "Rock and roll!" That's what they want to hear. But Bob wouldn't give in.

He said, "You wanna rock 'n' roll . . . You can go and see Kiss and you can rock and roll your way down into the pit."

Bob hoped his faith would bring him serenity and peace of mind. That didn't happen. In 1986 he married again, this time to an African American woman named Carolyn Dennis. She had been a backup singer in his band. They had a daughter, Desiree Dennis-Dylan. However, Bob's second marriage did not last. He and Carolyn Dennis were divorced in 1992.

Nothing seemed to work in Bob Dylan's life. Except the music. In fact he once said, "At times in my life the only place I have been happy is when I am onstage."

Chapter 11
Fifty Years and Counting

So who is Bob Dylan really?

In 2007, a movie came out about him called *I'm Not There.* Six different actors, including a woman and a young African American boy, all played Bob Dylan. That is probably as close to a "real" picture of Bob as anyone can get.

What he does give the public is his music.

In September 2012, Bob Dylan released *Tempest*, his thirty-fifth studio album. But unlike

many singers, he doesn't wait for a new album to go on tour. He likes to play concerts. In fact, he will play almost anywhere. Once Bob played at the United States Military Academy at West Point. One of his songs that night was the antiwar ballad "Masters of War."

Bob Dylan plays small towns and big cities around the country and all over the world. Fans call it "The Never Ending Tour." Not all of his albums have been as great as *Blonde on Blonde*. Still, he has won ten Grammy Awards, including two for Album of the Year. In 1988 he was inducted into the Rock and Roll Hall of Fame. The Hall also named five of his songs on a list of songs that helped shape rock and roll.

Bob Dylan has kept on trying new things in his music.

For a couple years, he belonged to a group called the Traveling Wilburys. He sang under the names Lucky Wilbury and Boo Wilbury.

DYLAN'S MUSICAL UNIVERSE

THROUGHOUT HIS CAREER, BOB DYLAN HAS SHARED THE STAGE WITH SOME OF ROCK'S MOST FAMOUS NAMES. HERE ARE SOME OF THOSE MUSICIANS.

AIMEE MANN
BRUCE SPRINGSTEEN
DAVE MATTHEWS
ELVIS COSTELLO
GEORGE HARRISON OF THE BEATLES
THE GRATEFUL DEAD
JACK WHITE OF THE WHITE STRIPES
JOAN BAEZ

BRUCE SPRINGSTEEN

GEORGE HARRISON

JOHNNY CASH

MARK KNOPFLER OF DIRE STRAITS

MICK TAYLOR OF THE ROLLING STONES

NEIL YOUNG

NORAH JONES

PATTI SMITH

PAUL SIMON

ROGER MCGUINN OF THE BYRDS

ROY ORBISON

TOM PETTY

BONO OF U2

VAN MORRISON

JOHNNY CASH

BONO

The other Wilburys were all rock superstars, too—George Harrison, Roy Orbison, Tom Petty, and Jeff Lynne.

Dylan has also acted in seven movies and directed two of them—*Renaldo and Clara* and *Eat the Document*.

In 2016, Dylan was awarded the Nobel Prize in literature. It was the first time in twenty-three years that an American had won the award.

Bob Dylan will always be a private person. But one hundred nights a year, he walks onstage with his Fender Stratocaster guitar.

Perhaps he remembers the magic a teenage boy in Minnesota felt when he played a Little Richard song on the stage at Hibbing High School. Or maybe he thinks about listening to the radio late at night, searching for the rock music that changed his life.

BOB DYLAN
ROCK AND ROLL
HALL OF FAME

TIMELINE OF BOB DYLAN'S LIFE

1941 — Robert Allen Zimmerman is born on May 24

1946 — His father catches polio, and the family moves to Hibbing, Minnesota

1959 — Graduates from high school and enrolls in the University of Minneapolis

1961 — Moves to Greenwich Village in New York City
Meets Woody Guthrie

1962 — His first album, *Bob Dylan,* is released

1963 — *The Freewheelin' Bob Dylan*, featuring the hit song "Blowin' in the Wind," is released
Plays with Joan Baez at the Newport Folk Festival
Performs at the March on Washington for Jobs and Freedom

1965 — Releases the hit song "Like a Rolling Stone"
Marries Sara Lownds

1966 — Jesse Byron Dylan, the first of his five children, is born
Blonde on Blonde is released
Suffers a motorcycle accident

1967 — The documentary *Don't Look Back* by D. A. Pennebaker is released

1968 — His father dies of a heart attack

1979 — Releases *Slow Train Coming*, an album dealing with Christian themes

1986 — Marries his second wife, Carolyn Dennis

1988 — Inducted into the Rock and Roll Hall of Fame

1998 — Wins Album of the Year Grammy for *Time Out of Mind*

2007 — *I'm Not There*, a movie about Bob Dylan, is released

2012 — President Barack Obama presents Dylan with the Medal of Freedom

2016 — Awarded the Nobel Prize in literature

TIMELINE OF THE WORLD

The United States enters World War II after Japanese war planes bomb Pearl Harbor on December 7	1941
World War II ends	1945
The state of Israel is created	1948
"Rudolph the Red-Nosed Reindeer," sung by Gene Autry, is a number one hit	1950
In *Brown v. Board of Education*, the Supreme Court declares that schools can no longer be segregated	1954
March on Washington for Jobs and Freedom President John F. Kennedy is assassinated	1963
Beatlemania hits the United States	1964
Martin Luther King Jr. is assassinated in April	1968
Apollo 11 lands on the moon The first Woodstock Festival takes place	1969
The Beatles officially break up	1970
President Richard Nixon resigns after scandals related to the 1972 Watergate break-in	1974
On July 4, the United States turns two hundred years old	1976
Saturday Night Fever, a movie about disco dancing, is a hit	1977
Sony introduces the Walkman, a portable music-cassette player, to the United States	1980
Sandra Day O'Connor becomes the first female Supreme Court judge	1981
The *Challenger* space shuttle blows apart shortly after takeoff	1986
Apple's iPod, a portable digital music player, is introduced	2001
Barack Obama takes office as the first African American president of the US	2009

BIBLIOGRAPHY

Dalton, David. **Who Is That Man?: In Search of the Real Bob Dylan**. New York: Hyperion, 2012

Dylan, Bob. **Chronicles: Volume One**. New York: Simon & Schuster, 2004.

Gray, Michael. **The Bob Dylan Encyclopedia**. New York: Continuum, 2008.

Marcus, Greil. **Bob Dylan: Writings 1968–2010**. New York: PublicAffairs, 2010.

Scaduto, Anthony. **Bob Dylan**. New York: Tolmitch Press, 2009. First published 1971 by Grosset & Dunlap. Kindle edition.

Shelton, Robert. **No Direction Home: The Life and Music of Bob Dylan**. 1986. Revised and updated edition. Edited by Elizabeth Thomson and Patrick Humphries. Milwaukee: Backbeat Books, 2011.